Barack
Obama

ABDO
Publishing Company

Buddy BOOKS
First Biographies

by
Sarah Tieck

VISIT US AT
www.abdopublishing.com

Published by ABDO Publishing Company, 8000 West 78th Street, Edina, Minnesota 55439.

Printed in the United States of America, North Mankato, Minnesota
092009
012010

 PRINTED ON RECYCLED PAPER

Coordinating Series Editor: Rochelle Baltzer
Contributing Editors: Heidi M.D. Elston, Megan M. Gunderson, BreAnn Rumsch, Marcia Zappa
Graphic Design: Jane Halbert
Cover Photograph: *White House Photo*
Interior Photographs/Illustrations: *AP Photo*: Alex Brandon (p. 27), Manuel Balce Ceneta, File (p. 22), Charles Dharapak (p. 28), Ron Edmonds (p. 21), Morry Gash, File (p. 25), Spencer Green (p. 24), M. Spencer Green (p. 17), Gerald Herbert (p. 28), Jae C. Hong (p. 26), Lawrence Jackson, File (p. 22), Pablo Martinez Monsivals, Pool (p. 5), Obama for America (pp. 6, 15, 16), Obama Presidential Campaign (pp. 6, 12), Seth Periman (p. 19), Punahoe Schools, File (p. 11); *PhotoDisc, Inc.* (pp. 9, 13).

Library of Congress Cataloging-in-Publication Data

Tieck, Sarah, 1976-
  Barack Obama / Sarah Tieck.
     p. cm. -- (First biographies)
  ISBN 978-1-60453-985-1
  1. Obama, Barack--Juvenile literature. 2. Presidents--United States--Biography--Juvenile literature. 3. Racially mixed people--United States--Biography--Juvenile literature. I. Title.
  E908.T54 2010
  973.932092--dc22
  [B]
                    2009031067

Table of Contents

Who Is Barack Obama?

Barack Obama is a famous **politician**. In 2009, he became the first African-American U.S. president. This made history.

Barack is also an author. He has written two books. One is called *Dreams from My Father*. The other is called *The Audacity of Hope*.

As president, Barack is the leader of the U.S. government.

Barack's Family

Barack Hussein Obama Jr. was born on August 4, 1961. He was born in Honolulu, Hawaii.

When Barack was young, he lived with his mother. His father moved away.

Barack's parents met in college. His mother was Ann Dunham. His father, Barack Obama Sr., was from Kenya, Africa. They divorced in 1964.

Ann married again. Barack's stepfather was Lolo Soetoro. In 1967, Barack and Ann moved to Lolo's home in Indonesia. Barack's younger sister Maya was born there. Later, Ann and Lolo divorced.

Indonesia is a group of islands in Southeast Asia. There, Barack realized that people live differently around the world.

Growing Up

When Barack was ten, he returned to Hawaii. Ann traveled often. So, her parents, Madelyn and Stanley Dunham, helped raise Barack and Maya. Barack became very close to them. He called them Toot and Gramps.

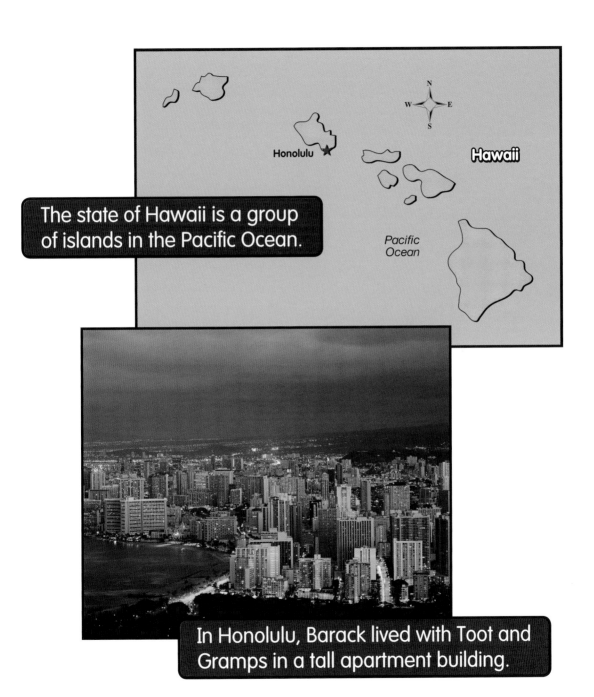

The state of Hawaii is a group of islands in the Pacific Ocean.

In Honolulu, Barack lived with Toot and Gramps in a tall apartment building.

In Hawaii, Barack attended Punahou Academy. There, he realized his skin color made him different. As one of three African-American students, Barack sometimes experienced **racism**.

Growing up, Barack was a talented basketball player. He was called Barry O'Bomber for his shooting skills.

Toot had been treated unfairly because she was a woman. But she didn't let it hold her back. Toot's strength inspired Barack to follow his dreams.

Higher Learning

Barack **graduated** from high school in 1979. Later, he studied **politics** at Columbia University in New York City, New York. He graduated from Columbia in 1983.

Barack knew learning would help him gain opportunities.

After college, Barack looked for a job helping people. In 1985, he took a job in Chicago, Illinois. He helped poor people who lived on the city's South Side.

UNITED STATES

Chicago
Illinois

Chicago is a large city. Barack worked to improve its struggling neighborhoods.

A Great Mind

Barack liked his work. But, he wanted to further his education. So in 1988, he entered Harvard Law School in Cambridge, Massachusetts.

People noticed Barack's hard work and good ideas. In 1990, he became the first African-American **editor** of the *Harvard Law Review*. And in 1991, he **graduated** with great honors.

After Harvard, Barack taught law classes in Chicago.

Starting a Family

Barack and Michelle make a good team. They have much in common.

In 1989, Barack had met Michelle Robinson. They had worked at the same law firm and became friends. Barack and Michelle stayed close while Barack was away at law school.

In October 1992, Barack and Michelle married. They lived near Michelle's family on Chicago's South Side. Later, they had two daughters. Malia was born in 1998. Natasha, called Sasha, was born in 2001.

Barack and Michelle are loving parents to Malia (*right*) and Sasha (*left*).

Visiting the Past

Before attending law school, Barack had traveled to Kenya. He visited his father's grave. Barack also met his other brothers and sisters there.

Barack wanted to tell his family's story. So when he returned home, he began writing a book. In 1995, *Dreams from My Father* was **published**. Readers noticed Barack's storytelling talent.

Barack's book sold many copies.

Making Changes

   Barack had always been interested in **public service**. In 1996, he became an Illinois state senator. He worked hard to improve life for the people of Illinois.

   In 2004, Barack gave an important speech at the **Democratic** National Convention. People were excited by his ideas and energy.

Barack is known for being a talented speaker.

Barack's family stood by him as he became a U.S. senator.

Senators work in Congress. They help make important laws and changes.

In 2005, Barack became a U.S. senator. He was the fifth African American to ever hold this office.

Then in 2006, *The Audacity of Hope* was **published**. People all over the world noticed Barack. Some thought he could become the next U.S. president!

Elected President

In 2008, Barack was chosen to be the **Democratic candidate** for president. He spent many months traveling to **rallies** and giving speeches.

Barack had many supporters during his campaign.

People were excited about Barack's ideas. In November 2008, Barack got the most votes. So, he was elected president!

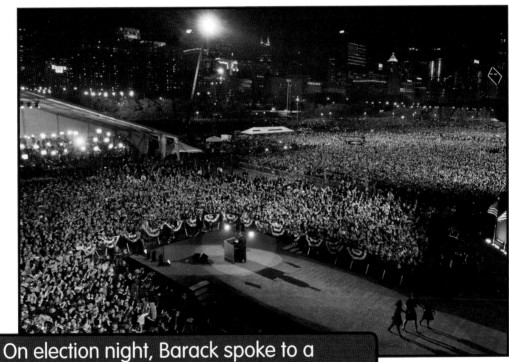

On election night, Barack spoke to a cheering crowd at Grant Park in Chicago.

Dream Come True

To become president, Barack took the oath of office. He promised to serve his country the best he could.

On January 20, 2009, Barack became the forty-fourth U.S. president. People around the world watched the event on television. More than 1 million people traveled to see it in person.

Barack and his family started a new life. They moved into the White House in Washington, D.C. In April 2009, the Obamas got a puppy named Bo.

On the night Barack became president, he and Michelle attended several balls.

As president, Barack meets with U.S. officials. They discuss issues concerning the United States.

Part of the president's job is to travel and give speeches.

Barack was excited to begin working as president. The United States was at war, and many Americans were out of work. Barack wanted to improve these problems.

Barack works hard for Americans. He visits other countries, makes many speeches, and directs the U.S. military. Barack Obama is hopeful about the **future** of the United States.

Important Dates

1961 Barack Obama is born on August 4.

1983 Barack graduates from Columbia University.

1991 Barack graduates from Harvard Law School.

1992 Barack marries Michelle Robinson.

1995 *Dreams from My Father* is published.

1996 Barack becomes an Illinois state senator.

1998 Malia Obama is born.

2001 Sasha Obama is born.

2005 Barack becomes a U.S. senator.

2006 *The Audacity of Hope* is published.

2009 Barack becomes the forty-fourth president of the United States.

Important Words

candidate (KAN-duh-dayt) a person who seeks a political office.

Democratic relating to the Democratic political party. Democrats believe in social change and strong government.

editor someone who prepares a publication, such as a newspaper or a magazine, for print.

future (FYOO-chuhr) a time that has not yet occurred.

graduate (GRA-juh-wayt) to complete a level of schooling.

politics the art or science of government. A politician works in politics.

public service work done to build a community or support its members.

publish to print the work of an author.

racism (RAY-sih-zuhm) the belief that one race is better than another.

rally an event during which people come together for a common purpose.

Web Sites

To learn more about Barack Obama, visit ABDO Publishing Company online. Web sites about Barack Obama are featured on our Book Links page. These links are routinely monitored and updated to provide the most current information available.

www.abdopublishing.com

Index